Hueber Lektüren

Sorrow

Philip Voysey

Illustrated by Elizabeth Botté

Hueber Verlag

This is the German version of **Sorrow**

Sorrow
Created and developed by
International Language Teaching Services Limited
Business and Technology Centre, Shire Hill
Saffron Walden, Essex CB11 3AQ UK

help@ilts.info
www.ilts.info

Author: Philip Voysey
Series editor: James Bean
Illustrations: Elizabeth Botté
Text design: ILTS Ltd

3. 2. 1. Die letzten Ziffern
2011 10 09 08 07 bezeichnen Zahl und Jahr des Druckes.
Alle Drucke dieser Auflage können, da unverändert, nebeneinander benutzt werden.
1. Auflage

Redaktion: Heike Birner
Umschlaggestaltung: Parzhuber & Partner, München
Umschlagfoto: © Das Fotoarchiv/Wolfgang Schmidt
Druck und Bindung: Ludwig Auer GmbH, Donauwörth
Printed in Germany
ISBN 978-3-19-802960-2 (Package)
81.2960 (Buch)

Contents

Chapter 1

The township

The bus arrived in the township of Chimuka as the sun was setting. Sorrow looked out of the window. People were moving about in the soft pink light – so many people, busily going somewhere. There were places to go and things to do in the town. Sorrow was sure of that. His stomach was churning. He felt anxious, but it was a good feeling. This was it – his new home. This was his future.

As the bus stopped, Sorrow looked at the people waiting outside. One of them was his uncle, but which one? He took the photo from his shirt pocket. On the back was the name of his uncle, Lovemore Mangwere. The photo showed a young man in the green and brown uniform of a freedom fighter carrying an AK-47 gun. He was tall and strong. The gun looked like a toy in his hand. But the war was more than twenty years ago. What did he look like now?

Sorrow stepped out of the bus into clouds of dust and the smell of diesel. He looked closely at the faces. None looked like his uncle. Maybe he hadn't waited. The bus was more than an hour late. But then, buses were always late.

Then he remembered his bag. The man who had collected the money on the bus was now on top of it, passing bags down to passengers waiting below. Everyone wanted their bag first. They all shouted up at him. 'No, the brown one!' 'The big suitcase!' 'Be careful of the pots!'

An old man reached up to take his bag and dropped it. The bag fell open and clothes spilled onto the ground. The old man sank to his knees and began gathering his clothes from the dust.

'Let me help you, old man,' Sorrow said.

'You're a fine boy. You don't live here, do you?'

'I've just arrived from the village.'

'Which one?'

'Mutubani.'

'A Mutubani boy, eh?'

The old man closed the bag and Sorrow helped him to his feet. The man straightened his hat and wiped the dust off his trousers. He took Sorrow's hands in his and said, 'Let an old man give you some advice. Make sure you stay a Mutubani boy. Don't let this place change you.' Then he smiled and walked away.

Sorrow watched the crowd gradually disappear. He turned to see a man coming towards him. He was smoking a cigarette and wore a long-sleeved shirt that hung over a big stomach. He was fatter and older than the man in the photo, but Sorrow recognised the face.

'You must be Sorrow,' said his uncle.

They shook hands in the familiar way, taking the hand, then the thumb, then the hand again.

'Welcome to Chimuka, the place where dreams come true!' Lovemore said, laughing. It was a strange laugh that made Sorrow wonder whether his uncle believed what he had said.

'Let me look at you. You're thin, aren't you? Your father told me to look for the boy who looked like a tall ripe stalk of corn.'

Sorrow wished the cornstalks in the village stood as straight and tall as he did. Too often they were short and bent over from a lack of rain.

'So, are you ripe? Are you ready to become a man?'

'I don't know,' Sorrow said.

'The first thing a man has to be able to do is drink. Do you drink?'

'No, Uncle.'

'Well, you're going to have to learn. We might as well start now.'

They walked down the street. Music was coming from

shops. Men cycled past ringing their bells. Women were cooking *sadza* in large pots by the side of the road. Sorrow loved the smell of the cooked corn flour. He loved the soft thick sticky feel of it in his hands. But most of all he liked the taste of it eaten with vegetables or meat and the heavy feel of it in his stomach. A man couldn't do anything without *sadza*.

It was night in the township now. Tall floodlights bathed everything in orange. Sorrow had never seen such huge lights. They were much bigger than normal streetlights.

'You like the floodlights? The white government put them up during the war,' Lovemore explained. 'They didn't want us boys to have any dark places to hide. That's what we freedom fighters were called – the boys.'

Sorrow knew about his uncle's life as a freedom fighter. He had led attacks on farms in the north of the country that changed the course of the war. He was known as a brave fighter.

'Now, *this* is the place where dreams come true,' Lovemore said, leading Sorrow into a beer garden that had a roof but was open on all four sides. You could enter or leave from any direction. Inside, men were sitting around tables drinking *chibuku*, the local beer made from corn. They drank from cartons. Lovemore found a table, then went and got two cartons of *chibuku*.

'Cheers to you. To life in the town.'

It tasted bitter.

'You don't like it?' said Lovemore.

Sorrow shook his head.

'Don't worry,' said his uncle. 'I'll drink yours.'

There was so much that Sorrow wanted to ask him. What was it like for a sixteen-year-old to fight in a war? Sorrow was the same age now as his uncle had been back then. He couldn't imagine what it was like to kill someone. But he couldn't ask that – not yet. And he wanted to know why Uncle had never returned to Mutubani in all the years since the war. He was a hero to people there.

Except to Sorrow's father. 'People call Lovemore a hero,' his father had said one day, 'but he has done terrible things – things he can never forget.'

His father would never say what those things were. When Sorrow said goodbye to him in the village he simply said, 'My brother is not like other men. If you decide you don't want to stay with him, I will understand.'

Sorrow and Lovemore walked through the streets. 'It's a bit different from Mutubani, eh?' said Lovemore. To Sorrow, the orange of the floodlights made the place look like a strange land where nothing was real.

After a while they came to a brick house and his uncle said, 'This is it.'

They went through a gate and along a path to the front door. Over the door hung the head of a snake. 'That's to scare thieves away,' Lovemore said. Then he led Sorrow inside, turned on the light and said, 'Welcome to my palace.'

They were in a room with a big couch and a big television.

'This is the living room,' said Lovemore. Then he stroked the smooth concrete floor and said, 'Look, no mud floors here. Not bad, eh? And this is how you watch television.' He used a remote control to turn the television on.

'Let's continue the tour.' They went into the kitchen. 'The refrigerator,' Lovemore said, 'with the necessities of life.' Inside it the shelves were filled with *chibuku*.

Then he turned on the tap and said, 'Put your hand under there.' Sorrow felt the water gradually get hotter.

'Come,' his uncle said, leading him through the house. 'One...two...three bedrooms. This one is yours.'

It was a large room with a bed, drawers and a table. A wire was suspended across the room for hanging clothes. Hanging on it was a green school uniform.

'I didn't want you to turn up to school tomorrow looking like a villager.'

Sorrow could barely hide his joy at the sight of the uniform. He wanted to shout out, but his father had taught him to control his emotions, especially when he was with respected elders.

'I think you've got everything you need,' Lovemore said. 'One last thing.' He led him down the corridor. 'This is the toilet and shower. Look, you can sit on the toilet.'

In Mutubani the toilet was a hole in the ground, and Sorrow was used to washing in the river. He couldn't believe his luck. This house was much more than he had imagined. This was the house of an important and successful man.

Later, when they were sitting on the couch eating *sadza*, his uncle explained, 'The government gave me this house after the war. A lot of the boys got big houses, good jobs, cars – our reward for making history.'

In his room that night, Sorrow tried on the uniform. It fitted perfectly. As he unpacked his bag – two shirts, long trousers, underpants, socks, one jumper, one pair of shoes, books and pens for school and a copy of the Bible his father had given him to read – he remembered the words of the old man. *Don't let this place change you.*

What did he mean? Sorrow wanted to change. He'd come to town so that he would never again have to dig soil as hard as rock or feel the sun burning his skin. Starting from tomorrow, he would become an educated man. The day was nearer now when he would sit in an office wearing a shirt and tie. One day when he went back to the village he would take money, lots of money, to his parents and two younger sisters. He would take them a television and all the wonderful things you could buy in town.

This was his future. He'd been blessed. As he went to bed

he could still feel the churning in his stomach. But he felt more excited than anxious. Tomorrow could not come soon enough.

Chapter 2

School

The sound of a car horn woke Sorrow. He got out of bed, took the uniform from the suspended wire and put it on. He walked past his uncle's room to the living room. A carton of *chibuku* was sitting on the floor. He went outside into the street. The light was pale and the air was cool on his skin. Women walked past carrying cooking pots on their heads and babies on their backs.

School started at seven. He didn't want to be late so he went back inside to check the time on the kitchen clock. It was just after six. He rubbed his shoes with a cloth to make them shine.

Just then, his uncle came in and said, 'You can't go to school without *sadza*.' He poured the dry *sadza* into a pot, added water and put it onto the stove to cook.

When it was cooked they sat down at the table, taking handfuls of the white, thick *sadza*, mixing it with meat and eating it.

'Chimuka is a good school,' said Lovemore. 'It was one of the first schools built after independence. I was the first deputy principal of the school. You didn't know that, did you?'

Sorrow shook his head.

'The government gave me the job after the war. But I didn't stay in it long. It didn't suit me. I don't belong in an office. I'm better with a gun than a pen.' He laughed, then suddenly went quiet. His eyes had a far-away look.

'Enough of the past,' he said. 'You'd better get to school. I'll see you when you get back.'

Sorrow walked along dusty streets, past square mud brick houses with iron roofs that were rounded and grey like an elephant's back. Suddenly he came to an open area and saw the red brick buildings of the school. His stomach began to churn again – he was looking at his future.

A large crowd of students was gathered in the assembly area at the front of the school. Sorrow felt alone. He didn't know anyone. He stood and watched their conversations, their laughter, the way they held each other's hands as they talked.

He thought of his best friend from the village, Mugove, and the day they had come across an elephant as they were wandering through the corn field on the way to the river. They frightened the huge beast away with sticks and loud screaming. After that day they became inseparable friends. They had conquered fear together. Sorrow wondered when he would see Mugove again. He wished his friend were with him now.

The class lists were on a large board at the side of the assembly area. Sorrow found his name in Class 1A just as several teachers appeared at the front. Suddenly everyone went quiet.

A teacher called out names and classes, and the students formed into groups. Sorrow joined his class – 1A. He looked along the row of students. He was older and much taller than most of them, like a giraffe standing above all the other animals. Students behind were laughing at him. If only his father had sent him here three years earlier. But Sorrow knew it had taken his father years of extra work in the village to raise the money to get him here.

A group of students sang the national anthem, *Simudzai Mureza Wedu WeZimbabwe*. It was a song of freedom, a song of hope. They sang beautifully, the deep voices of the boys harmonising with the higher voices of the girls. Sorrow wished he were singing with them.

A teacher told the students to sit on the ground, and then the principal spoke to them about the behaviour he expected.

'I expect you to be punctual. Your uniforms should be neat

and clean. You must respect your teachers at all times. Work hard. There is no future without hard work. Lazy people do not go anywhere in this life.'

Hearing these things made Sorrow smile. This was how a school should be.

1A's first subject was History, in Room 10. Sorrow entered the classroom and took a seat at the front. A blackboard covered almost the entire front wall.

A teacher wearing a suit and tie walked in. All the students stood up.

'You can sit down. I am not the president,' he said, laughing. 'I am not even the principal. My name is Mr Sibanda.'

He looked at the students and asked, 'What do you know about the history of this great nation?'

No one said a word.

'You don't have to be frightened of me. What about you?' he said, looking at Sorrow. 'Tell me something.'

Sorrow immediately regretted sitting at the front.

'We gained our independence through war, teacher.'

'Yes, good. Freedom in this country was won with blood and courage. It was won with people fighting together.'

Mr Sibanda moved around as he spoke, making his hands dance as if he were performing. Sorrow couldn't take his eyes off him. He listened hard, trying to take in every word, hungry for knowledge.

That first class went quickly. Sorrow felt inspired. He left the classroom wanting to know more about his country's history. None of his other teachers that morning had the same energy or the same ability to make their lessons interesting.

School was over by midday. As Sorrow was leaving, the students for the afternoon school from twelve o'clock to five o'clock were just arriving.

He wandered past women selling nuts that had been boiled

in salty water. The smell made his mouth water. He could hear music coming from the direction of the market. He stopped for a moment to listen. It was a Thomas Mapfumo song. Sorrow loved the melodies of the guitars. He started to dance and then realised where he was. He looked around, but no one had seen him. He continued on his way home, singing to himself as he walked.

Chapter 3

Two worlds

Sorrow was surprised to arrive home to an empty house. His uncle had said he would be there when he got back.

He went into his room and changed his clothes, hanging his school uniform neatly over the wire. He went to the kitchen. There was left over *sadza* and meat in the refrigerator, but the right thing to do was to wait for his uncle to return, so he went into the living room, sat on the couch and turned the television on. There were pictures of houses being bulldozed, leaving nothing but bits of tin and wood on the ground. Watching the big machine destroy the houses was like watching an elephant flatten a field of corn. The difference was that you couldn't frighten a bulldozer. Women were crying as they watched their homes being bulldozed. Men were shouting angrily as police pushed them away. A government minister was talking about building better houses for the poor.

It wasn't long before Lovemore walked in through the door.

'Ah, my young nephew, how was your first day at school? Did your future fly down from the sky like an eagle and carry you away? The claws of the future are so sharp. They tear the flesh. They make you bleed.'

It was a strange thing to say. Sorrow could smell the *chibuku* on his uncle's breath. He had been drinking. And from the red in his eyes, Sorrow could tell he'd been drinking a lot.

Sorrow told him about Mr Sibanda and the History class.

'Did you tell him your old uncle was a war hero?' Uncle asked.

Sorrow shook his head.

'You didn't tell him I rescued this country from the whites?'

Sorrow said nothing. You couldn't talk to a person who

had been drinking. Uncle sank into the couch.

'Did he tell you how the struggle gave us nothing but false hope? How everything we won has been lost? How this country has no future? The corn is dying in the fields. Dying in the fields, my young Sorrow. Now there are empty stomachs and broken dreams.'

Lovemore went to the refrigerator and took out a bottle of beer. He held it up and laughed. 'This is my dream. This is all I have.'

Then he pulled the top off the bottle with his teeth and spat it out.

That night Sorrow lay awake in bed thinking about his uncle's drinking. Drinking was a curse. Drinking turned good men bad, made gentle men violent. He'd seen it in his village – men who had drunk too much coming home and beating their wives and children, then feeling sorry the next day for what they had done and begging for forgiveness. Because of this, his father had never allowed alcohol in the house.

Sorrow also thought about the things his uncle had said. Was it true this country had no future, or was it the alcohol talking? Alcohol made sensible men say stupid things. Sorrow believed that he had a future – a bright future. That was the promise of education – a good job that paid good money. Wealth meant success, and success meant happiness. This much he was sure of.

Before he went to sleep he read a few verses from the Bible and said a few prayers. He prayed for the health of his family. And he prayed for his uncle. He prayed that whatever evil spirit had entered his body would leave him in peace.

In the days and weeks that followed, Sorrow began to live in two worlds. There was school, where hope and inspiration shone brightly on each day. In Mr Sibanda's classroom he learnt about great African chiefs – Dingiswayo, Mzilikazi, Shaka Zulu, Lobengula – and how the lives of the dead breathed in the living. He learnt that freedom wasn't a gift, that it was only won through giving blood and only kept with sweat, tears and more blood.

When he wrote letters home to his parents, he wrote about this world. He didn't write about the other world – the darkness of the house, his uncle's drinking and negativity, his lack of faith in the future.

Sorrow decided it was best to keep out of his uncle's way. He got into the habit of coming home from school, having *sadza* for lunch and then studying while Lovemore was out drinking and the house was quiet. When Lovemore returned in the late afternoons Sorrow would go down to the market, a place of activity and noise where people sold everything from fruit and vegetables to clothes and watches. Sorrow loved the market. All the goods were laid out on the stalls. He was amazed at all the calculators, mobile phones, CD players and television sets. He wondered how anyone in a poor township such as Chimuka could afford to buy these things. Maybe, like him, they came to look and dream.

He loved the smell of fresh herbs and cooked corn. The sound of guitars roared from loudspeakers filling every corner of the market. Women moved their hips as they shopped. Children danced. One man selling beans was always too busy playing his guitar to serve his customers. When Sorrow heard the music, his mood became light and cheerful and he forgot about his uncle and the darkness of the house.

Chapter 4

Honesty

Saturdays and Sundays were the worst days for Sorrow. School brought purpose to each day. Without it, he wasn't sure what he was supposed to do. Having a free day was something new to him. Back in the village there was always work to be done in the fields.

Being several years older than all the other children in his class had made it difficult for him to make friends. Since his uncle spent most of his time at the beer garden, Sorrow had become used to spending weekends on his own, doing his homework and trying to improve his reading. He read the Bible and a book of African folk tales he'd borrowed from the school library.

One Saturday a boy about Sorrow's age turned up at the house. He wore a T-shirt with a picture of Ronaldo, the great Brazilian football player, and a Nike cap over hair that was cut almost to the skin of his head. But the most noticeable thing about him was his smell. It was bad – it reminded Sorrow of the pigs back in Mutubani.

Lovemore introduced him as Honesty Mariwa.

'Some kids call me Ronaldo,' Honesty added.

'I invited Honesty over,' Lovemore said. 'I was thinking you needed a friend. I've asked him to show you around.'

Sorrow and Honesty wandered to the market together.

'You like Ronaldo?' Sorrow said.

'He's the best. I want to be like him one day. I want to be the best football player in the world.'

'You'll have lots of money.'

'Too much!' Honesty said. 'So, you go to school?'

'Don't you?' asked Sorrow.

'No. I left last year. I've got no time for school.'

'How come?'

'School can't put food on the table,' he said. 'Hey, if you had as much money as you wanted, what would you buy?'

'Too much,' Sorrow said. A nice shirt for his father, a cool pair of sunglasses for his friend Mugove, one of those electric pots for cooking *sadza* for his mother and some books for himself.

'I'd buy a yacht and sail the Mediterranean. I'd have satellite TV so I could watch football all day. That's the life.'

The market was up ahead. It was packed with people. Honesty led Sorrow along one of the narrow passageways between the stalls. They squeezed through the crowd of people and came out the other side.

'Let's go over there. I want to show you something,' Honesty said, leading Sorrow away from the market.

He took a small box out of his pocket and gave it to Sorrow. Sorrow opened the box. Inside was a calculator.

'It's for you. You can use it at school,' Honesty said. 'I've got something else,' he said, and took a wallet from his other pocket. He opened it and took out the money – sixty dollars.

'Not bad,' he said with a smile, then he threw the wallet under a car parked nearby.

'You stole these things,' Sorrow said.

'Of course.'

Sorrow looked at the calculator. He could certainly use one for school. But he couldn't keep something that was stolen.

'You should take it back.'

'Are you crazy? They'd beat me.'

'But you can't steal. It's wrong.'

'If you haven't got a job you have to steal. That's the way it is. It's easy. I can teach you how.'

Sorrow had no intention of learning how to steal. 'I think I'd better go back,' he said.

'Hey, you think it's bad to steal? Well it's not as bad as going hungry. You know what it's like to go without *sadza* for three days?'

'No.'

The thought was unimaginable. His family had often gone without meat and sometimes without vegetables, but they'd always had *sadza*.

'Your stomach aches. Your whole body cries out. You'll do anything for *sadza* – beg, steal – it doesn't matter. You'd do the same. Anyone would.'

Sorrow was sure he'd beg before he'd steal. Begging didn't hurt anyone else.

'You know it was Rambo who taught me how to steal,' said Honesty.

'Who's Rambo?'

'Your uncle. He was the best. He could do markets, buses, trains, shops. He even did a bank once. But he got too old. You have to be quick with the fingers. You have to be able to get away fast. So he got a group of us kids to work for him. He taught us how to steal and we gave him part of what we earned. Now I work alone.'

Sorrow was too shocked to say anything.

'He asked me to teach you. If you like, we can work together, until you're good enough to work on your own.'

Sorrow shook his head. 'I'd better go.'

'Hey, what are you going to do when you finish school?'

'Get a good job in an office.'

'It's not going to happen. There aren't any good jobs. You're going to have to take a risk just to survive. You've got to think big.'

Sorrow didn't go straight back to the house. He wandered along the streets of elephant-back houses. In front of one house a woman was sweeping the dust, making it neat and tidy. Sorrow had always wondered why they bothered to do that. Dust rose, only to settle again in almost exactly the same place.

He wondered what he would say to his uncle. He had been taught to respect his elders. You could not argue with an elder. You could not tell him he was wrong. Besides, Lovemore was a war hero. But how could a hero become a drunk and a thief – and worse, get boys to steal for him? And how could Lovemore imagine that Sorrow would want to become one of those boys, that he could become a thief?

As he approached the house he felt that churning in his stomach. He thought of his father who had sacrificed so much for him. No, he couldn't walk away and return to the village.

'God, give me the strength and wisdom to say and do the right thing,' he said quietly to himself.

Chapter 5

A difficult choice

Lovemore was lying on the couch when Sorrow got home. As usual, he had been drinking.

'So, how was your day with Honesty?'

Sorrow had been preparing himself for this conversation. He knew he had to be strong but respectful.

'Fine.'

'Honesty knows the township. He can show you around, teach you things.'

What, how to be a thief? Sorrow thought.

'So, where did you go?'

'To the market. Honesty stole a calculator and a wallet.'

Lovemore laughed. 'Eee! He's a clever boy. He has eyes like the eagle. He sees his prey, swoops, then disappears on the wind. He's a good boy.'

'He said you taught him how to steal.'

'He learned from the best. You could learn too.'

'I don't want to learn to steal.'

'You might have to.'

'What do you mean?'

'Well, you see, my dear Sorrow, I'm running out of money.'

'But my father sent you money to pay for my costs.'

'Your father has no idea how expensive it is to live in Chimuka. You see, in Chimuka when you buy a new pair of trousers, they already have holes in the pockets. The money just pours out like sand. And you can't sew them up. It's impossible – I've tried. My dear Sorrow, if you want to stay you will have to earn some money. Or else ask your father for more.'

Sorrow certainly couldn't ask his father for more. He knew that his father had sent Lovemore a lot of money – several thousand dollars. It should have been enough for him to live in the township for years, not months. Sorrow suspected at least some of the money had been spent on drink, but surely not all of it. Where had the rest gone?

'Look, it's easy money,' said Lovemore. 'There's not much risk if you do it right. Think of it as pocket money.' He laughed again.

'I can't steal. It's wrong.'

'Ah, you have principles. You believe in doing the right thing. Principles are fine if you are rich. But when you are poor, you have no choice – you can't afford to have principles. You have to be like the hyena. You have to take what you can. Principles don't fill your stomach, my dear Sorrow.'

'I plan to get a good job.'

'Ah, yes. If wishes were horses, beggars would ride. Let me tell you something, Sorrow. There are no jobs. We have become a country of beggars. We hold out our hands to the world and cry, "Help us, help us." Everything the government promised us after the war has come to nothing. Where is the land we were promised? The whites still have it. Government ministers have it. The promise of land for the people has dried up and died, like the corn. It's nothing but dust. Promises don't fill stomachs. I fought, I killed for nothing. For nothing, my dear Sorrow.'

'But you fought for our freedom. You were a hero,' Sorrow said.

'A coward, not a hero. I was scared. Everyone was scared. But you do anything to live.'

His voice lowered almost to a whisper.

'Sometimes you do things you wish you hadn't. Things that make you ashamed.'

'I don't understand.'

'There are some things I hope you never understand. Things I'd rather forget.'

Sorrow was curious. What were those things?

After a long pause Lovemore said, 'Sorrow, you have a choice. If you want to stay here and continue at school you'll have to find some money from somewhere. I don't have enough to support you any more. If you can't support yourself, then you'll have to go back to the village. And now, I'm off to heaven.'

He picked up his jacket and left. Sorrow watched him walk out of the gate and turn towards the beer garden.

Sorrow sat on the couch. He turned the television on and then turned it off again. Who was his uncle then – hero or thief, good man or bad? Maybe all of those things.

But one thing was clear to Sorrow. There was no future for him back in the village. He had to stay here with his uncle. So he had to find money from somewhere. He would study harder than he ever had before. He would do so well at school that no one could refuse him work.

Chapter 6

The thief

On weekends Sorrow looked for work. His uncle had given him a month to find a job. First he tried the shops in the township. He asked every seller in the market if he could help out. He even went to the clothes factory out of town. But everywhere he went he got the same story. Not only was there no work, but a queue of people in front of him who also wanted work.

When this failed he went to the town of Madoma, five kilometres away. He went to every shop there.

The owner of one shop told him, 'If everyone who had asked me for work stood in a line, it would go out of this door and all the way to Chimuka. I'm telling you, man, these are hard times, very hard times. If things don't get any better I'll be closing this shop and going down to South Africa.'

As the end of the month approached, Sorrow had no idea where or how he was going to get the money he needed. Uncle and Honesty were right. There was no work. So what was the point of school? What was the point of staying at Chimuka? But to go home to the village would be to admit defeat. That would be to give up on a dream. The words of Honesty came back to him – *Take risks. Think big.*

He went down to the market one Saturday morning. He found Honesty kicking around a football with young kids. He was wearing his Ronaldo shirt. Sorrow watched him from a distance – the way he controlled the ball, the way he could beat a defender by going around him, through him or over him. He was skilful and quick on his feet. Honesty dribbled the ball around five boys, before letting the very smallest boy, who was no more than four or five, take the ball off him.

'Eee! You are too good,' he said with a grin. 'After me, you're the next Ronaldo!' he said, picking up the boy.

'Hey, Honesty,' Sorrow shouted.

They shook hands.

'Don't you ever take that shirt off?' asked Sorrow.

'No. It's good luck. Ronaldo always scores. He's quick. He's fast. He never gets caught – like me. You want to play?'

'No.'

'So, what's up?'

'I want you to teach me to steal,' Sorrow said.

It was the hardest thing he'd ever had to say. But what choice did he have? He knew it was wrong. But didn't the Bible say thieves would be forgiven? And this would only be for a short time. It was the only way he could help himself and his family.

Honesty grinned. 'Okay. You can be Ronaldinho. We'll work together.'

The next week, after school, Honesty showed Sorrow how to use two fingers to remove a wallet from a pocket. He showed him how to use a knife no bigger than his little finger to cut through bags. He demonstrated the importance of working in crowds, how there was less chance of being caught.

At the end of that week, Sorrow was to put these new skills into practice. He had hardly slept all week. He had prayed for forgiveness every night before going to bed.

On Saturday, Honesty came to the house in the morning and together they went to the market. It was crowded as usual. Sorrow had a sick, sinking feeling in his stomach.

'I don't think I can do this,' he said.

'Hey, Ronaldo and Ronaldinho – unbeatable! Come on, it's easy. Wait for my signal. I'll nod my head like this when I'm ready. I'll steal the wallet and hand it on to you. All you have to do is walk out of the market with it. Just act normally.'

First, they watched people as they moved through the market, to see where they kept their money. The idea was to choose someone who kept their money in a back pocket or bag, somewhere easy to get at with fingers or a knife.

Honesty chose their prey quickly. A man was moving between the stalls with a wallet almost falling out of his back pocket. Honesty nodded his head and followed him. Sorrow felt strangely excited. This was a big risk. He didn't know what was going to happen. It was like facing up to the elephant with Mugove.

They walked behind the man as he pushed his way through the crowd. The music was loud. Sorrow felt himself being pressed between bodies. They pushed forward until they were hard up against the man. For a moment, no one was moving. A moment was all Honesty needed. Sorrow didn't see his friend at work. He suddenly felt the wallet being pressed into his hand. He put it into his front pocket, fought his way to the edge of the crowd and headed back in the direction they had come.

They met up again outside. Sorrow handed the wallet to Honesty.

'Fifty,' said Honesty. 'Not bad. You take twenty.'

Sorrow took the twenty-dollar note. He examined it closely. It was old and well used and a little torn. But it was still twenty dollars.

'Let me see the wallet,' said Sorrow. 'I want to know who the man was.'

'It's better not to,' said Honesty.

'I want to.'

Sorrow took the wallet. Inside was a plastic card showing the face of the man. His name was Joseph Mafindi. He looked about forty. Old enough to have a family. Old enough to be a husband and father with a responsibility to put food on the table every day. Sorrow wondered how many children were depending on him.

ALDO

'He's ugly. Look at that jaw. He looks like a rhino,' said Honesty.

Sorrow couldn't help but laugh. Suddenly he imagined the man with a horn instead of a nose. He handed the wallet to Honesty and said, 'You'd better throw this away.'

Then he folded his twenty-dollar note carefully and put it in his pocket.

'Let's try the bus station,' Honesty said.

As they walked towards the bus station, the music from the market still in their heads, Sorrow felt that churning in his stomach. He had taken the jump. There was no turning back now.

Chapter 7

The guitar

Sorrow and Honesty became a skilful team. At first Honesty did the stealing and handed the money on to Sorrow to make the escape. But Sorrow was a quick learner, and within weeks he was as fast and skilful as his teacher.

They continued to work the market and bus station, anywhere where a crowd was gathered. On Saturdays they started early, so that they could be at the bus station at seven, when the crowds gathered for the longer bus trips to the big cities of Harare in the north and Bulawayo in the south. Every Saturday was the same – people leaving the township for the day or the weekend, attracted by the promise of money to be made in the city. There were women with sacks of corn flour on their heads and pots on their hips, off to set up a cooking stall and sell *sadza*. There were men with sacks of clothing and shoes, others with electrical goods such as mobile phones, CD players and calculators.

Starting early also meant that Sorrow and Honesty could finish in time to be at Chimuka Stadium by three o'clock in the afternoon to watch the local football game. Nothing got in the way of Honesty seeing the game, not even the need to make money.

After several weeks of staying in the township, they started working the bus from Chimuka to Madoma. The crush of people, the bumping and pressing of bodies against each other, made it easy to steal wallets without anyone noticing. The other thing in their favour was that it was only a short five-kilometre journey with a number of stops along the way. When one of them got a wallet, he would signal to the other with a nod of the head and they would get off at the next stop.

Sorrow spent his weekends going back and forth on the bus with Honesty. They split whatever money they stole. On a good weekend they might get as much as a hundred dollars. Sometimes they got as little as ten. It depended on how much money was in a wallet and how many chances they got to steal.

Sorrow gave half of whatever he stole to his uncle and kept half for himself. That was the understanding he had with him. As long as he did that, he could stay in the house and continue to go to school during the week. The money he gave to Lovemore paid for food. Sorrow suspected that it paid for his beer as well. Sorrow used some of his half to pay for pens, and boiled nuts on the way home from school. The rest he hid in a tin at the back of one of his drawers. He planned to use the money to buy gifts to give to his family when he returned to Mutubani at the end of the year.

Having his own money made Sorrow feel in control of his life for the first time. He depended on no one. The boy from Mutubani was becoming a man.

It wasn't that he thought stealing was right – there was still a part of him that felt shame each Saturday morning when he met Honesty at the bus station. But when they got on a bus, all doubts disappeared.

One Sunday Sorrow returned to the house to find his uncle in his familiar position on the couch, the television on, a beer in his hand.

'The hyena returns,' he said. 'How much have you got for me today?'

Sorrow pushed ten dollars into his hand.

'Is that all?'

'No luck.'

'What can I buy with ten dollars?'

'*Sadza*.'

'No, I need more than this,' Lovemore said, taking Sorrow by the arm. He held him tightly. For the first time Sorrow felt afraid of his uncle. He could smell the beer on his breath. He wanted to escape to his bedroom but Lovemore would not let go.

'That's all there is.'

'No, no, no. You must be keeping something from me. Show me what's in your pockets.'

He showed his uncle the ten dollars he was keeping for himself. When Lovemore saw it, he grabbed it and said, 'So what's this?'

Sorrow didn't know what to say. His uncle knew he always divided the money.

But Lovemore spoke angrily. 'You want to stay here and all you have for me is ten dollars? Well, the cost of living is going up, up, up. I need at least fifty dollars next time, or you'll have to leave. Understand? Fifty dollars.'

Sorrow escaped to his room. He was shocked. He had seen a new side to his uncle – a hard, cruel side. His uncle meant what he said.

He lay awake that night wondering how he would meet his uncle's demand.

That week he forgot to hand in a History essay. Mr Sibanda pulled him aside after class.

'What happened? You never forget an essay.'

'I just forgot. I'll hand it in to you tomorrow, teacher.' Sorrow turned to leave.

'Is everything okay?'

'Sure, teacher.'

'Your uncle is looking after you?'

'Yes, teacher.'

'Look, Sorrow, I know what sort of a man your uncle is. He's a drunk. He spends his days at the beer garden. Everyone knows that.'

'He's a war hero, teacher.'

'He *was* a war hero. He worked here at the school for a while and then left. Then he started running a gang of child thieves. He must have had ten kids working for him. Everybody in Chimuka knew what he was doing. The police didn't arrest him because he was one of "the boys". And because he paid them.'

Sorrow bowed his head in shame. He hadn't realised that everybody in the township knew the kind of man his uncle had become.

After school, Sorrow decided to take a longer way home. He needed time to think.

He wandered down an unfamiliar street and came across an open rubbish tip. There was usually something useful in a rubbish tip, so he went to have a look. Something shiny and blue caught his eye. He looked more closely. It was the flat body of an electric guitar. He picked it up. A big piece was broken out of it where the neck should be. But he liked the metallic blue colour. He looked around for the neck and found it sticking out from under a piece of plastic. He put the body on the ground and put the neck in place. The two pieces fitted together. All it needed was some bolts screwed into the back of the body and into the neck.

But why would anyone throw away a good guitar? It was probably no good. He put it back on the tip and started walking home.

He'd only walked a short way when he turned around and went back to the tip. He picked up the broken pieces. He wasn't sure what he would do with it, but he couldn't leave it there. Maybe he could fix it up and sell it. Maybe he could learn to play it. That was an idea. The thought warmed him as he wandered home.

Chapter 8

Some promises

The next day Mr Sibanda surprised the class by bringing in a guitar and taking them to sit under the jacaranda tree at the back of the school.

'Songs were part of the freedom struggle,' he said. 'Songs help people to remember the past and imagine the future. Songs speak to our hearts and souls. We can sing about our fears and hopes and dreams.'

Then he started playing. He sang songs of freedom. He sang songs about the hard life of a freedom fighter.

It's hot out here
And I thirst for the beer
Back home where life was easy
But I'm stuck with the flies
And the crocodile eyes
By the banks of the wide Zambezi

Sorrow laughed. He imagined his uncle thirsting for beer. But after a while, he no longer heard the words. All he could hear was the rhythm and melody of the guitar. He couldn't take his eyes off Mr Sibanda's fingers moving quickly up and down the neck. It was like a dance between the left and right hands. It seemed that each finger had its own intelligence and was acting independently, yet knew what the others were doing. Sorrow wanted to be able to do that.

After the class he approached Mr Sibanda.

'Teacher, can you teach me to play the guitar?'

'Sorrow, you need discipline to learn the guitar. I'm not sure you have that discipline. Look what's happened to your schoolwork.'

It was true Sorrow's schoolwork had got worse as a result of his weekends spent with Honesty. He often handed his homework in late, and the quality was not as good as it had been at the beginning of the term. He just didn't have as much time any more.

'But I want to learn.'

'To learn the guitar you have to play every day for at least half an hour. Can you do that? If you can't, it's a waste of time.'

'I can.'

'Do you have a guitar?'

Sorrow told him about the broken guitar he'd found in the rubbish tip.

'Bring it in and I'll see if I can fix it for you. But if I'm going to teach you, I want some promises from you. First, I want you to promise me you'll hand in all your homework on time. Can you do that?'

Sorrow nodded.

'Second, I want you to promise me you'll stop spending time with Honesty Mariwa. I know what you two do together and I want it to stop. Can you make that promise?'

Sorrow's head went down. He wanted the earth to open up and swallow him. How did Mr Sibanda know? Did people talk? And if so, how many other people knew him as a thief? What did people think of him as he walked down the street? Sorrow had thought he could keep his two lives separate.

'So, can you make that promise? I don't want you ending up in a prison. I can't teach you the guitar in there.'

Sorrow nodded, but he kept his head down.

'No. That's not good enough,' said Mr Sibanda. 'I want to see it in your eyes and I want to hear you say it. Look at me, Sorrow.'

Sorrow lifted his head slowly.

'Tell me what you are not going to do.'

'I'm not going to see Honesty Mariwa again.'

'What else?'

Sorrow knew what he wanted him to say, but he couldn't

say the words, because to do that was to admit what he had become. It was to admit that stealing was not just something he did on weekends to earn money, like some kind of hobby. It was not just an adventure. It was more than that. The act of stealing had changed who he was. It had poisoned his soul.

'What else, Sorrow?'

Sorrow looked into the eyes of his teacher. He saw kindness and strength.

'I'll never steal again.'

'Good. Bring me the guitar tomorrow.'

Chapter 9

Honesty's fate

On the Saturday morning, Sorrow woke not knowing what to do. His continued attendance at school depended on him getting the extra money his uncle wanted. But how was he going to get it if he didn't steal? The two demands of his uncle and his teacher were pulling him in different directions.

He didn't eat breakfast. He left the house before Uncle woke, and headed towards the market.

An old man in a brown suit, tie and hat cycled past. He smiled at Sorrow. It was a smile he'd seen somewhere before. Then he remembered. It was the old man he'd seen at the bus station that first day. He remembered those words. *Make sure you stay a Mutubani boy. Don't let this place change you.*

Sorrow repeated the words to himself. He had changed. But was the Mutubani boy gone forever, or was he still there inside him?

Mr Sibanda had told him not to see Honesty, but he couldn't just walk away from his friend without saying anything. He liked Honesty. He was the only friend he had made in the township.

Sorrow found Honesty playing football outside the market. Once again he was entertaining the other children with his skill. Sorrow didn't go up to him immediately. He watched him play. Suddenly Honesty stopped and stood with the ball under his right foot.

'Come and get the ball,' he said to three of the children.

When they came towards him he dribbled around them and scored.

'Goal!' he shouted, pulling his shirt over his head and running with his arms above his head like the star he wanted to be one day.

Mr Sibanda was wrong. Honesty was definitely not bad. Perhaps the promise Sorrow had made was wrong too. It was better to break a promise than walk away from a friend.

Honesty saw Sorrow and came over to him.

'Where were you this morning?' he said.

'I've got a problem,' said Sorrow. He explained the situation with his uncle but he said nothing about the conversation with Mr Sibanda.

'Rambo wants fifty? Then we need two hundred,' said Honesty. 'Why don't we try Harare? People have more money in the city.'

Sorrow had been to Harare once with his father as a child. He could remember the tall buildings and cars, but that was all. The idea of going there again excited him.

He decided to spend one last day with Honesty. After this, he would never steal again.

At Chimuka bus station there was the familiar rush of people trying to get onto the buses heading out of town. All in a hurry, all demanding immediate attention from the men on the roofs of the buses who were busy with the baggage.

Bus horns sounded above the music coming from loudspeakers. This added to the urgency and crush of people around the buses.

It was a perfect opportunity for Honesty and Sorrow. They didn't need to say anything to each other. They joined one crowd of people pushing to get onto a bus. Sorrow was close behind Honesty. It wasn't long before he felt a wallet being pushed into his hand. He then made his escape, pushing through the crowd, seeking cover behind a nearby shop.

Suddenly there was a commotion. He heard a man shout, '*Tsotsi! Tsotsi!*' – 'Thief! Thief!' and he froze. He turned back and saw two men pull Honesty from the crowd. They started punching him. They punched him to the ground and started kicking him. Honesty curled up in a ball and covered his head.

He cried out for the men to stop, but they kept kicking him.

'Stop kicking the boy,' one woman shouted.

'He's a thief,' one of the men said, kicking Honesty again. 'And there's another one around here somewhere.'

Hearing that, Sorrow took the money out of the wallet he was holding, threw the wallet away and started running as fast as he could. He ran along dusty streets, not thinking about where he was going. He ran until he felt as if his chest were about to explode. When he eventually stopped, he was in a part of the town that he didn't know. He stood on a street corner, catching his breath.

Suddenly he felt guilty at having left his friend at the mercy of those men. No one would think anything of killing a thief. He had to go back and see if Honesty was okay. Friends stuck together. Hadn't he and Mugove frightened the elephant away by acting together?

He retraced his steps as best he could until he was able to hear the music coming from the market. He headed towards it. Then when he got near the bus station he stood out of sight at the side of a shop and watched.

There was no commotion, and no sign of Honesty – only people pushing to get on buses. After a while he built up the courage to move closer. There was a stain of blood on the ground where Honesty had lain. His heart sank. He checked the waiting room and the bus station toilet, but there was no sign of Honesty. Then he walked the short distance to the health centre, thinking he might have been taken there. But the nurses hadn't heard of him. No boy had been brought in for treatment.

If only he knew exactly where Honesty lived. He knew he lived somewhere on the edge of the township where the poorest people lived in houses made out of thin bamboo poles, with dirt floors and no electricity or running water. Sorrow had never asked to go there and Honesty had never invited him. There were some things – some parts of yourself – that you didn't want others to see.

Sorrow headed home, hoping that Honesty was safe in his own bed, but suspecting something much worse. He felt light, as if his body were empty, like a balloon floating through the air. He wished a wind would pick him up and take him all the way to Mutubani.

Chapter 10

Uncle's secret

'Ah, my young hyena, back so soon?' said Lovemore as Sorrow came in. 'How much have you got for me?'

Suddenly Sorrow was angry. For months he'd given his uncle respect, because that was what his father had taught him to do. No matter how bad a person Lovemore was, he was still his uncle. But in that moment of anger, respect meant nothing.

'I've got nothing for you!' Sorrow shouted, his whole body shaking. 'Nothing!'

'Eee, you shouldn't speak to your uncle like that.' Lovemore spoke calmly, and this angered Sorrow more.

'I hate you,' Sorrow said, and spat on the floor.

'Ah, you might hate me, but you need me.'

'I wish you were dead.'

Lovemore started laughing. 'That's funny. So do I! We both want the same thing. Why don't you kill me right now and put an end to this miserable life?'

He got up and went and got a large knife from one of the kitchen drawers. He gave it to Sorrow. 'Do it. Please. I would have done it a long time ago, but I'm a coward, remember? I don't have the courage to kill myself.'

Lovemore grabbed Sorrow's hand and pulled the knife towards him so that the point rested against his stomach.

'Go on. Do it! Stab me! Hard!'

Sorrow went cold with fear. His hands were trembling.

'Don't be a coward,' said Lovemore. 'You hate me. It's easy. What's my life worth? I'm a drunk and a thief. I'm worse than a dog. Do it!'

As Lovemore pulled the knife harder, Sorrow began to cry. 'I can't.'

'Let me make it easy for you. Let me tell you what sort of

man your uncle is. I haven't told you, have I? How I killed a family in cold blood? A white family. A father, a mother, two children. Innocent people.'

Lovemore's voice started to tremble. Sorrow could see the tears in his eyes.

'I remember the black farm worker shouting, "Don't shoot them." He said they were good people and didn't deserve to die. But I had hatred in my heart. I had to make someone pay for a hundred years of us being treated worse than dogs. So I made them kneel down and then I shot them – bang! And you know what? I didn't feel a thing. When you hate as much as I did, you don't feel pity. It was war.

'But just when you think you've forgotten, memories come back. It's like having hyenas tearing at your insides. There's not a day when I don't relive that moment. I hear their cries. I see their faces. Can you imagine what that's like, to see their faces every day? Do you want me to live with that? Do it. Please. I'm begging you.'

'I can't.' Sorrow was barely able to say the words. Lovemore relaxed his hold on Sorrow's hand and Sorrow dropped the knife.

Sorrow went straight to his room. He gathered his things and quickly packed his bag. He reached for the tin of money at the back of the drawer and opened it. He froze in shock. The tin was empty. There had been over three hundred dollars in it. His uncle had taken everything.

Sorrow walked straight out of the house without looking at him, without saying a word.

He had forty dollars from the wallet he and Honesty had stolen. It was enough to get a bus back to Mutubani. The only problem was that it was now late in the afternoon. There were no more buses heading towards Mutubani. He headed to the market and went straight to a food stall where a woman was serving *sadza* and meat sauce. He sat down to eat.

When night fell, he went to the school. It was the only place he could think of where he would be safe from the drunks who walked the streets late at night. He put on every item of clothing he had, and although he still felt the cold, he curled up into a ball outside Room 10 and fell asleep.

Chapter 11

A second chance

The morning sun was a deep orange. It reminded him of the mornings in the village where he would rise with the sun to begin a day's work in the fields. He would be there soon.

He set off towards the bus station. As he came to the first corner, he turned around to take one last look at the school. The brick buildings shone with the warmth of the sun. He realised he would probably never see that school again. He had no choice but to return to Mutubani.

He arrived at the bus station to find that passengers were just beginning to gather. His bus was due to leave in an hour, so he wandered over to the market for *sadza*.

'Sorrow.' He heard a familiar voice, and just for a moment he half-expected to see Honesty. But it was Mr Sibanda, leaning his bike up against a nearby stall.

'What are you doing here so early?' Mr Sibanda asked.

'Eating *sadza*.'

'Why aren't you eating at home?'

Sorrow didn't want to tell Mr Sibanda the shameful story. He lowered his eyes and said nothing.

'Are things okay with your uncle?'

'Yes.'

'Are you sure?'

Sorrow nodded.

'Okay,' said Mr Sibanda, but he didn't sound convinced. 'I've got a surprise for you. I've repaired that guitar and put strings on it. Why don't you finish your *sadza* and come to my house? We can have our first lesson.'

'I can't. I'm catching a bus.'

'You look as if you're going for a long time. Have you got clothes in the bag?'

Freunde des Braunschweiger Botanischen Gartens e.V.

Pelargonien-Hybride: „Brunswik“
(Pelargonium-Grandiflorum-Hybride)
Foto: Klaus Baeske

Sorrow nodded.

'Where are you going?' Mr Sibanda asked.

Suddenly Sorrow felt all the emotion of the past few days rushing to the surface. Tears filled his eyes and ran down his cheeks. He lowered his head. He'd been taught that men didn't cry, certainly not in public. But there was nothing he could do to stop the tears.

'Come on, let's go somewhere else,' Mr Sibanda said, picking up the bag and putting it on the back of his bike.

They walked a short distance through the township until they came to a small brick house with a flat tin roof. Sorrow followed his teacher inside and sat on a couch. There was a poster of Bob Marley on one wall and Thomas Mapfumo on another.

'My heroes,' Mr Sibanda said, pointing at the two famous musicians. He sat beside Sorrow. 'Tell me what happened.'

Sorrow explained the whole story. It was a relief to be able to talk about everything that had happened. For months now, anger and confusion had weighed heavily on him. As he spoke, he felt the weight lifting. He still felt anger towards Lovemore, but the hatred was gone. Instead Sorrow felt pity for what his uncle had experienced and what he had become. Then when he spoke about Honesty, he was overcome with sadness and tears poured out of him. And there was the guilt of having left his friend to such a terrible fate.

'You were right to run. You couldn't have saved him. You had to save yourself,' Mr Sibanda said.

'Do you think he's dead?'

'No, probably just badly beaten. I'll ask around if anyone knows what happened to him. So, what are you going to do?'

'Go back to the village. There's no future for me here.'

'You're wrong. There is a future if you keep fighting for it. That's what the history of this country tells us. Hey, I was going to show you this.'

Mr Sibanda went into another room, and then came back with the blue electric guitar and another one. The blue one had been fixed. He gave it to Sorrow.

Sorrow ran his fingers across the strings, making a soft sound that disappointed him.

'It's not much use without amplification,' Mr Sibanda said, attaching a lead to the guitar and plugging it into a small amplifier.

'Now try it,' he said.

Sorrow ran his fingers across the strings again. This time the sound was loud, filling the room.

'Wow!' said Sorrow.

'You want me to show you what it can do?'

Mr Sibanda took the guitar and began to play, his left hand moving smoothly up and down the neck while his right hand plucked the strings, playing melody and rhythm at the same time.

'I want to be able to play like that,' Sorrow said.

'You will. It takes time.'

Mr Sibanda gave the guitar back to Sorrow. He tried to play like his teacher had, but he couldn't make a clean sound. He wasn't playing music – he was making noise. He shook his head.

'This is hard.'

'The fingers just have to learn to dance together. First we need to do some exercises to make them flexible and fast. I'll play my guitar and you follow me.'

Mr Sibanda played the first four notes on the bottom string – first finger, second finger, third finger, little finger then back to third finger, second finger, first finger. He played slowly, but Sorrow still found it difficult to keep up. They went up and down the first string and then moved to the other strings in turn. It was difficult to make the notes and pluck at the same

time. It wasn't long before his left hand began to ache and his fingers became sore.

'I'll never be able to play like you.'

'Of course you will. Half an hour each day, that's all it takes. It's a shame you're going back to the village. I won't be able to teach you.'

'I'd stay if I could, but I've got nowhere to live.'

'You don't know anybody else in Chimuka?'

Sorrow shook his head.

'Well, why don't you stay with me until we find somewhere else for you to live? I've got a spare room. We could have guitar lessons every night. I'll talk it over with the principal. I'm sure it will be okay. What do you think?'

Sorrow's face lit up. He could barely hide his joy. He wanted to hug his teacher but of course he couldn't. That would have been disrespectful. Instead he smiled and nodded.

'I take that as a "Yes".'

As he sat up in bed later that night, Sorrow said a prayer for the first time in weeks. He thanked God for Mr Sibanda. He had a second chance to make something of his life and it was all because of him. Yesterday all had appeared lost. Suddenly everything was possible again.

Chapter 12

The Stardusters

By October the clear skies of the previous nine months had disappeared. Each morning clouds gathered, becoming blacker as the day wore on, before bursting around mid-afternoon, sending everyone rushing for cover and transforming dusty streets into muddy pools. At night, electrical storms flashed across the sky. The rain brought a smile to Sorrow's face because he knew that back in Mutubani his family would be celebrating.

It was perfect weather for studying and playing the guitar. Sorrow worked hard at school and did his homework in the afternoons. If he went to the market, it was only to buy fruit or vegetables or peanuts. He always looked out for Honesty but he never saw him.

Sorrow lived for the nights, for that moment after they had eaten *sadza* and washed the dishes, when he and Mr Sibanda would pick up their guitars and play.

At first progress was slow. Sorrow had to force his fingers to move, but it wasn't long before they began to move by themselves. Soon he could accompany his teacher on simple songs, playing the rhythm while his teacher played the melody. He discovered that the guitar had its own personality, depending on how you played it. It was like having a new friend.

One night Mr Sibanda suggested that they start up a school band.

'You know a few songs – enough to get started.'

The next day Mr Sibanda stood up in front of the school at assembly and announced that he would be forming a school band. Anyone who was interested was to come and meet in

Room 10 on Saturday morning, with instruments if they had them. 'We'll see who can do what,' he said.

Only seven students turned up on Saturday, some from morning school and some from afternoon school. Apart from Sorrow there was another boy, Dennis, who played the guitar. Like Sorrow, he had come with an electric guitar that had been broken and then fixed. He wore a white beret on his head. It made him look like a musician.

Another boy, Ahmed, came with a drum kit made from bits and pieces from the rubbish tip – old tins of different sizes with plastic stretched across them for drums, a foot pedal that barely worked to beat the drums, and the lids off the tins for the cymbals.

Wadznayi and Tabeth, two girls better known for their skills playing netball, offered themselves as back-up singers along with two boys, David and Takesure.

It was Dennis who took the lead. He plugged his guitar into Mr Sibanda's amplifier and started playing. The melody was familiar – a song, *Angelina*. Sorrow couldn't take his eyes off Dennis's fingers moving up and down the neck of the guitar effortlessly. He made it look so easy. The four singers burst into song.

Angelina come on down…

Sorrow started playing the rhythm while Dennis played melody.

When the song had finished, Dennis went straight into another song. He played *Kilimanjaro, No Woman No Cry* and some other songs. They were all songs everyone could play and sing along to. Within half an hour they were playing together as a band. By lunchtime they had worked out harmonies and the guitar parts to ten songs. The four singers had even started to work out simple dance routines.

Mr Sibanda sat back and listened as the band began to take shape.

'You sound great. I don't need to do anything! So what are you going to call yourselves?'

Sorrow and the others looked at Dennis. They all recognised him as their leader. He was the best musician by far. He was the one who knew the songs.

'The Stardusters,' he said.

Sorrow walked home with Mr Sibanda. He could barely contain his excitement.

'Dennis is fantastic,' he said.

'He plays very well. He can teach you a lot.'

'Do you think it's possible for me to become a great guitar player?'

'Sure, if you work hard enough.'

'I think that's what I want to do. Play music. Be in a band.'

'There's a saying – "A man's reach should exceed his grasp, or what's a heaven for?" If you have a dream, there's no point leaving it by the side of the road or throwing it on the rubbish tip. You must throw it into the air like a balloon and then see if you can catch it. Just don't forget your schoolwork, okay?'

Sorrow practised every night. Mr Sibanda would play Dennis's melody part while Sorrow played rhythm. They played late into the night.

By the following Saturday, Sorrow knew the songs well. This time Ahmed came with a proper bass drum, one that had animal hide instead of plastic and produced a much deeper sound. He'd also found a foot pedal that worked.

They rehearsed for three hours, although Sorrow hardly noticed the time passing. He was too busy concentrating on his guitar playing. Playing music emptied his mind of all else. It made time stand still.

After a month of practising, they were ready to perform. One Monday Mr Sibanda announced to the school that The Stardusters would give a free concert at the end of morning school the following Monday.

The students let out a long 'Eeeeee!' of delight. Hearing this reaction made Sorrow's stomach jump. There was no turning back now. In a week's time he would be playing in front of more than a thousand students. He would either fall or fly into the sky.

Chapter 13

Doubt

In the week leading up to the performance, Sorrow found it difficult to think of anything else. He sat in class going over the songs in his head. He used his ruler as an imaginary guitar, playing the notes and chords up and down the twelve-inch neck. He saw himself standing on stage with the other members of The Stardusters.

When he practised with the band, hours passed in minutes. It wasn't just the playing that was fun. It was the conversation, the light-hearted joking between songs that bound them together as a group. For the first time since he'd come to Chimuka, Sorrow felt as though he belonged.

Dennis was the quiet leader. He was also the one who made everyone laugh. When he told Tabeth, Takesure, Wadznayi and David that they were singing like elephants and moving like hippos everyone fell about laughing. On another occasion he put dirty clothes in Ahmed's drum kit as a gentle reminder not to play so loud.

But when Dennis hit the first note of a new song, everyone became serious. Dennis used his eyes to signal approval or disapproval at what the others were doing. Narrowing the eyes meant you'd lost the beat and had to get it back fast. Opening the eyes wide meant you were playing okay.

At night Sorrow played the songs over and over again. He played them until the songs came as easily to him as the air that he breathed, until they were a part of who he was.

On the Sunday night before the big day, Mr Sibanda came into his room and said, 'It's sounding good. You sound ready.'

Sorrow smiled.

'The whole school is excited. Everyone is talking about The Stardusters.'

'I'm nervous. What if I make a mistake?'

'If you make a mistake, don't stop. Just keep playing. The audience won't even know you've made one. Play with joy and love in your heart and you'll be fine. I have to go early in the morning to organise the sound system. I just wanted to say good luck.'

On the Monday morning Sorrow woke to the chorus of bus horns from the nearby bus station. He reached down beside his bed, picked up the guitar and started playing the first song, *Angelina*.

He only got a short way into the song before he made a mistake. He went back and tried again, and this time made a different mistake. The third time, he made a mistake with the very first notes of the song. He tried the second song, and the same thing happened. He couldn't play without making mistakes, mistakes he'd never made before. His fingers that had been as light as dancers suddenly felt heavy and stiff.

He put down the guitar and got up from the bed. He wasn't ready after all. If he played he was surely going to make a fool of himself in front of more than a thousand students. Nothing could be worse.

'Mr Sibanda,' he called out.

There was no answer. Of course not – he'd left early.

Sorrow needed to talk to Dennis. He ran to school so that he could be there when Dennis arrived. He stood at the back of the assembly area and looked for him. When he saw the familiar figure carrying his guitar, he ran towards him.

'Dennis, I don't think I can do this. I can't play. I'm not ready.'

Dennis looked at him without changing his expression. The only thing that ever caused Dennis to show emotion was someone playing out of time or singing badly.

'Okay. We can play without you. It won't sound as good, but we can do it.'

Then he turned away and kept walking.

'I'm really sorry,' Sorrow called.

Dennis didn't turn back.

Sorrow was shocked. Dennis didn't care if he played or not. He hadn't even tried to convince him to play. Sorrow should have been happy that the band would go on without him but he wasn't. He was now more disappointed in himself than ever.

He sat in class with a sick feeling in his stomach. The feeling got worse as the morning went on and he had to excuse himself from his English class. He only just got to the toilet in time before being sick. He went back to the class, asked to be excused and went home.

He walked the long way, along streets scattered with pools of water. The rain had made everything damp and heavy. Dust, like all his hopes and dreams, had turned to mud. He heard the music from the market. He could never play music like that, he told himself. Never.

When he reached Mr Sibanda's house he went straight to his room and sat on the bed. The guitar leaned against the wall. He looked at it. He touched the neck and went to pick it up, then took his hand away.

He thought of his father, mother and sisters back in the village. What would they think of him now? They would be disappointed in him. Yes, of course they would. His father had sacrificed everything to give him an opportunity. And now an opportunity had come – a big one – and he was going to let it pass. Why? Because of fear. Fear of what? Fear of looking foolish? And yet he had overcome fear before. He and Mugove had looked the elephant in the eye and scared it away.

He could resist no longer. He picked up the guitar and started playing. 'Nothing to fear. It's okay to make mistakes,' he told himself.

He played *Angelina*, *Kilimanjaro* and *No Woman No Cry*. He played them perfectly. No mistakes, his fingers dancing lightly over the strings.

It was eleven fifty-five. He had five minutes to get to school.

Chapter 14

The concert

Sorrow ran all the way. He arrived as the students were gathering in the assembly area for the concert. Dennis and the other Stardusters were standing to one side while Mr Sibanda checked the sound.

'I'm going to do it,' Sorrow said to them. There were slapping hands all around. Dennis smiled at him, but said nothing.

Suddenly there was quiet in the assembly area as Mr Sibanda took the microphone and said, 'The Stardusters.'

As they walked out, the assembly exploded with cheers, whistling and ululating, tongues going from side to side in appreciation. The crowd got louder as Dennis played the introduction to *Angelina*, then became quieter as The Stardusters got into the song.

At the end of *Angelina* the cheering exploded again. The band looked at each other in disbelief. Dennis nodded his head and they went straight into *Kilimanjaro*. With the first notes of the song, Sorrow turned his concentration to the music, and the audience seemed to disappear. He kept one eye on his left hand on the neck of the guitar, the other on Dennis, at the same time listening hard to what the others were doing.

Again the audience burst into loud applause. Sorrow had never experienced anything like this. Over a thousand people were cheering. He felt important for the first time in his life.

At the end of the concert Mr Sibanda took the microphone again and shouted, 'The Stardusters!'

The students cheered and ululated and then the most remarkable thing happened. The students started throwing money. The Stardusters stood in disbelief as money rained

down around them – silver twenty and fifty cent coins and gold dollar coins.

'I think they liked you,' Mr Sibanda said as the assembly broke up.

'When's the tour?' Dennis joked.

'Well, you could give a concert in the township,' Mr Sibanda said. 'This money will pay for the sound, and maybe even a few posters.'

As he was heading home, Sorrow noticed a crowd of people who had been listening outside the school. His uncle was among them. Suddenly Sorrow's mood sank. He tried to pretend he hadn't seen him, but his uncle came after him.

'I heard the performance,' he said. 'You were good. Very good. Nice guitar.'

Sorrow turned to walk away.

'Hey, hey, don't go. I just came to say sorry.' He pushed an envelope into Sorrow's hand and said, 'The money I borrowed.'

'I don't have anything to say to you.'

'That's okay. Maybe one day you'll forgive me. I'm a sick man, Sorrow. You can't be angry at a sick man. Remember, I'm family.'

Sorrow walked away. On the best day of his life he resented his uncle even being there.

Chapter 15

Mutubani boy

That whole week, the talk in the school was all about The Stardusters. When Sorrow walked around the school he saw students pointing at him and heard them calling out the name of the band. Teachers treated him with new respect. He was no longer the boy who worked in the fields of Mutubani. He was a musician. Music lived in him and he wanted to share it with others. Music was his power, his gift.

Sorrow now had even more reason to practise hard. When he wasn't at school, eating or sleeping, he was playing his guitar. He carried it to school and played it in the break. He took it to the market and tried to play along to the music coming from the loudspeakers. On Saturdays he practised with the band in preparation for the concert in the township that Mr Sibanda was busy organising.

One night he took a rest from the guitar and sat beside Mr Sibanda in front of the television. A news report showed farmers in the fields talking about the corn crop.

'Your father's a farmer, isn't he? How are things with him?'

In truth, Sorrow hadn't written to his parents in months. First it was leaving his uncle's house that stopped him writing. He didn't know how he could tell them such news. And then it was the guitar, taking up almost every waking moment.

'I understand how important music has become for you,' Mr Sibanda said, 'but don't forget your parents. Don't forget where you come from.'

'But I never want to go back. Working in corn fields is no life.'

'It's a hard life, that's true. But what your father does is important. You can't play the guitar without *sadza* in your stomach.'

'But all I want to do is play music.'

'That's good. But just remember most people don't make a living from music. Certainly not in this country.'

'Are you saying I should give up?'

'No, you should practise with all your heart and soul. You should practise to become the best guitar player this country has ever seen. Better than Thomas Mapfumo or Oliver Mtukudzi.' He paused and turned off the television. 'Did you see your uncle the other day?'

'Yes.'

'I told him you were performing.'

'You did?'

'Yes. I hoped he'd come. It's good that he did.'

'I didn't talk to him. I don't want to talk to him. Ever.'

'Maybe some day you will. Even your uncle has decency in his heart.'

On Saturday Sorrow went down to the local stadium to see Chimuka play Chinoiya. There were dark clouds in the sky. Sorrow hoped the rain would stay away, at least until after the game.

During the game he walked around the football field, looking closely at the faces in the crowd. He hadn't lost hope of seeing Honesty – hadn't lost hope that he would suddenly appear and everything would be all right. Why not? Things had turned out well for Sorrow. He had lost his way and found his dream. If there was fairness in the world, if there was a God that looked after people with good hearts, then Honesty Mariwa was alive and well somewhere.

Suddenly there was a commotion. A snake had come onto the field. Players suddenly forgot the ball and set upon the snake, jumping up and down on it until it was dead. The flattened snake was then removed so that the game could continue.

The interruption changed the game. Down by one goal, Chimuka lifted their game and scored two late goals to win the game. The victory meant they would play in the finals for the first time in four years. Afterwards people joked that the snake had been Chimuka's twelfth man.

'We couldn't have won without the snake,' Sorrow heard one man say.

'We should make the snake a life member of the club,' said another.

Sorrow headed home. He passed the bus station and came to the join of two roads. Children were jumping over pools of water and throwing mud at each other.

Normally he took the road to the right that led home to Mr Sibanda's. But this time he stopped. He looked left, along the road that led to places he'd tried to forget. All of a sudden his stomach was churning.

He could walk away without looking back. That would be easy. But no matter how good the future looked, you could never forget the past. There were things in the past he needed to set right. He didn't want to live with resentment in his heart.

There was a loud crack of thunder followed by hard rain. People were scattering in all directions. Sorrow hesitated for a moment, and sheets of rain wet him through to his skin.

He started running towards his uncle's house.

Activities

Chapters 1, 2 and 3

Before you read

A. Look at the picture on page 5 and circle the correct answers.

1. Where are these people?
   a. at an airport b. in a car park c. at a bus station
2. What is the man on the bus holding?
   a. a white basket b. a brown suitcase c. a black hat

B. Find these words in your dictionary. Use them in the sentences.

freedom fighters churning township floodlights

1. My stomach was ______________ when I went into the exam.
2. Unlike the noisy city, the small ____________ is quiet at night.
3. We now have ______________, so we can play football at night.
4. The ___________ want to defeat the government and the army.

C. Listen to Track 3 on CD 1 and answer these questions.

1. When did the white government put up the floodlights?
   a. during the war b. last year
2. What were the freedom fighters called?
   a. the dreamers b. the boys
3. What was the local beer made from?
   a. corn b. cartons

After you read

COMPREHENSION

A. Circle the correct answers.

1. What were the floors of Lovemore's house made from?
   a. mud b. wood c. concrete
2. Why did Sorrow move to Chimuka?
   a. to go to school b. to start a job c. to join the army
3. What time did school start?
   a. seven o'clock b. eight o'clock c. nine o'clock
4. What was the big machine that destroyed houses called?
   a. a television b. a refrigerator c. a bulldozer

B. Circle T for true or F for false for these sentences.

1. Sorrow was fourteen years old. T / F
2. A head of a snake hung over Lovemore's front door. T / F
3. Lovemore was the first deputy principal of the school. T / F
4. Lovemore thought that the country had no future. T / F

C. Complete these sentences.

1. The old man said, 'Don't let this place ______________.'
2. The men drank *chibuku*, the local beer, from ______________.
3. For Sorrow, school was over by ______________.
4. Before he went to sleep, Sorrow said a few ______________.

D. Write short answers to these questions.

1. Who gave Lovemore his house after the war?

   ____

2. What book did Sorrow's father give him to read?

   ____

3. What was the name of Sorrow's history teacher?

   ____

4. Where did Sorrow go in the late afternoons when Lovemore returned?

   ____

Language activities

A. Use these words to make compound words from Chapters 1, 2 and 3.

1. town	room
2. flood	speakers
3. class	ship
4. loud	lights

B. Use these letters to make words from Chapters 1, 2 and 3. The first letter is given for each word.

1. nksea: s______________
2. lphnteea: e______________
3. rffgiae: g______________
4. gleae: e______________

What do you think?

Listen to Chapters 1, 2 and 3 on the CD. How was life different for Sorrow after he moved to the township of Chimuka?

____

Chapters 4, 5, 6 and 7

Before you read

A. Look at the picture on page 31 and circle the correct answers.

1. What are both boys holding?
   a. books b. money c. food
2. What do you think they've been doing?
   a. shopping b. studying c. stealing

B. Find these words in your dictionary. Use them in the sentences.

hyena principles beggar wallet

1. Rob has strong ______________. He'll never do anything that he believes is wrong.
2. I paid for my meal, then put my _________ back in my pocket.
3. The ______________ is a wild animal that looks like a dog.
4. The ______________ sat outside the station asking for money.

C. Listen to Track 4 on CD 1 and answer these questions.

1. How old was Honesty?
   a. much older than Sorrow b. about Sorrow's age
2. What was the most noticeable thing about Honesty?
   a. his clothing b. his smell
3. Who did Honesty want to be like one day?
   a. Ronaldo, the football player b. Lovemore, Sorrow's uncle

After you read

COMPREHENSION

A. Circle the correct answers.

1. What would Sorrow buy for his father if he had a lot of money?
   a. a shirt b. sunglasses c. some books
2. How much money had Sorrow's father sent Lovemore?
   a. several hundred dollars b. one thousand dollars
   c. several thousand dollars
3. How long did Lovemore give Sorrow to find a job?
   a. a day b. a week c. a month
4. At first, how much of the money Sorrow stole did he give to his uncle?
   a. none of it b. half of it c. all of it

B. Circle T for true or F for false for these sentences.

1. Honesty still went to school. T / F
2. Lovemore taught Honesty how to steal. T / F
3. Honesty was a bad football player. T / F
4. Mr Sibanda knew that Lovemore was a drunk. T / F

C. Complete these sentences.

1. Honesty said if you don't have a job you have to ___________.
2. Lovemore said, 'If wishes were horses, beggars ___________.
3. In a crowd, there was less chance of a thief being ___________.
4. Sorrow found the broken guitar in an open ______________.

D. Write short answers to these questions.

1. What did Honesty call Sorrow's uncle Lovemore?

   ____

2. What place did Lovemore call heaven?

   ____

3. Who taught Sorrow to steal?

   ____

4. Who made Sorrow realise that the whole township knew the kind of man his uncle had become?

   ____

LANGUAGE ACTIVITIES

A. Match each word with its opposite from Chapters 4, 5, 6 and 7.

1. right	poor
2. rich	bad
3. hero	wrong
4. good	coward

B. Write the missing vowels to make words from Chapters 4, 5, 6 and 7.

1. str _ ngth	3. r _ sp _ ns _ b _ l _ ty
2. w _ sd _ m	4. r _ sp _ ct

WHAT DO YOU THINK?

Listen to Chapters 4, 5, 6 and 7 on the CD. Do you think Lovemore is a good man or a bad man – or both?

____

Chapters 8, 9, 10 and 11

Before you read

A. Answer these questions about the story so far.

1. What was Sorrow going to do with the money he'd saved?
   a. buy clothes b. give it to his uncle
   c. buy gifts for his family
2. How much money might the boys get on a good weekend?
   a. ten dollars b. a hundred dollars c. a thousand dollars

B. Find these words in your dictionary. Use them in the sentences.

soul independently in cold blood curled up

1. On Saturday morning it was raining, so I ______________ in bed with a good book instead of going out.
2. The escaping prisoner shot the bus driver ______________.
3. They prayed for the ______________ of the man who drowned.
4. Some parents want their children to stay at home forever, but other parents can't wait for their children to live ___________.

C. Listen to Track 5 on CD 1 and answer these questions.

1. How many times had Sorrow been to Harare?
   a. once b. twice
2. How did Sorrow feel about going to Harare again?
   a. anxious b. excited
3. Where did Sorrow seek cover after he got the wallet?
   a. behind a nearby bus b. behind a nearby shop

After you read

Comprehension

A. Circle the correct answers.

1. What did Sorrow ask Mr Sibanda to teach him?
   a. how to steal b. how to play guitar c. how to drink beer
2. What does the word '*tsotsi*' mean in English?
   a. bus b. money c. thief
3. How much money was missing from Sorrow's tin of money?
   a. over three dollars b. over thirty dollars
   c. over three hundred dollars
4. Who found Sorrow at the market before he caught his bus home?
   a. his teacher b. his uncle c. his friend

B. Circle T for true or F for false for these sentences.
1. Sorrow promised Mr Sibanda he'd never steal again. T / F
2. Sorrow had made many friends in the township. T / F
3. Lovemore once killed a family in cold blood. T / F
4. Mr Sibanda lived in a house made of bamboo poles. T / F

C. Complete these sentences.
1. Mr Sibanda said songs were part of the freedom ____________.
2. Sorrow knew that friends stuck ______________.
3. Lovemore said, 'I don't have the courage to kill ____________.'
4. Bob Marley was one of Mr Sibanda's ______________.

D. Write short answers to these questions.
1. What had got worse as a result of Sorrow's weekends spent with Honesty?

   ____
2. What day of the week was it when Honesty was caught stealing?

   ____
3. Where did Sorrow go when night fell after he decided to leave his uncle's place and go home?

   ____
4. Whose house did Sorrow stay in after he left his uncle's house?

   ____

LANGUAGE ACTIVITIES

A. Circle the correct verb forms in these sentences.
1. We can **sing** / **sang** about our fears and hopes and dreams.
2. Sorrow **had been** / **will have been** to Harare as a child.
3. His hands **was** / **were** trembling.
4. Sorrow **don't** / **didn't** want to tell Mr Sibanda the shameful story.

B. Write the missing vowels to make words from Chapters 8, 9, 10 and 11.

1. r _ m _ mb _ r
2. _ m _ g _ n _
3. kn _ w
4. th _ nk

WHAT DO YOU THINK?

Listen to Chapters 8, 9, 10 and 11 on the CD. Do you think that Sorrow will make the most of his second chance?

____

Chapters 12, 13, 14 and 15

Before you read

A. Look at the picture on page 61 and circle the correct answers.

1. Where are these musicians performing?
   a. at the school b. at the market c. at the beer garden
2. How many people are playing guitars?
   a. one b. two c. three

B. Find these words in your dictionary. Use them in the sentences.

hide resented burst into dance routine

1. The child ____________ tears when she dropped her ice cream.
2. This rug is very unusual. It's made of zebra ______________.
3. Our new ______________ is difficult to learn but it will look great when we get it right.
4. Bill ______________ having to let his sister use his computer.

C. Listen to Track 6 on CD 1 and answer these questions.

1. When did Sorrow and Mr Sibanda play their guitars?
   a. during the day b. at night
2. Who suggested that they start up a school band?
   a. Mr Sibanda b. Sorrow
3. When was the meeting about the school band going to be held?
   a. Saturday morning b. Sunday morning

After you read

Comprehension

A. Circle the correct answers.

1. In which month did the storms and rain start?
   a. October b. November c. December
2. What reason did Sorrow give Dennis for not playing?
   a. His guitar was broken. b. He wasn't ready.
   c. He had to go home to the farm.
3. What was in the envelope Lovemore gave Sorrow after the concert?
   a. a letter b. a bus ticket c. money
4. What took up almost all of Sorrow's waking moments after the concert?
   a. doing his schoolwork b. playing the guitar c. sleeping

B. Circle T for true or F for false for these sentences.

1. Ahmed played the bass guitar. T / F
2. Dennis tried to convince Sorrow to play. T / F
3. Students threw money after the concert. T / F
4. Sorrow resented his uncle for coming to the concert. T / F

C. Complete these sentences.

1. After a month of practising, they were ready to ___________.
2. After the rains, dust turned to ______________.
3. After the concert, Mr Sibanda took the microphone and shouted, '______________!'
4. In the week after the concert, teachers treated Sorrow with new ______________.

D. Write short answers to these questions.

1. Who was the leader of The Stardusters?

   ____

2. Once Sorrow decided to play after all, how long did he have to get to school?

   ____

3. What was the first song The Stardusters played in the concert?

   ____

4. What came onto the football field and caused a commotion?

   ____

LANGUAGE ACTIVITIES

A. Match the words that go together in Chapters 12, 13, 14 and 15.

1. back-up	kit
2. electric	system
3. drum	singers
4. sound	guitar

B. Write the missing vowels to make words from Chapters 12, 13, 14 and 15.

1. f _ rm _ rs	3. m _ s _ c _ _ ns
2. t _ _ ch _ rs	4. st _ d _ nts

WHAT DO YOU THINK?

Listen to Chapters 12, 13, 14 and 15 on the CD. Do you think that Sorrow will forgive his uncle? Do you think that he should?

____

Glossary

adj. adjective; *adv.* adverb; *n.* noun; *v.* verb

amplification /ˌæmplɪfɪˈkeɪʃn/ *n.*	Verstärkung
amplifier /ˈæmplɪˌfaɪə/ *n.*	Verstärker
anxious /ˈæŋkʃəs/ *adj.*	ängstlich, besorgt
assembly /əˈsembli/ *n.*	Versammlung, Zusammenkunft
balloon /bəˈluːn/ *n.*	Ballon
bamboo /ˌbæmˈbuː/ *n.*	Bambus
beggar /ˈbegə/ *n.*	Bettler, -in
beret /ˈbereɪ/ *n.*	Baskenmütze
Bible /ˈbaɪbl/ *n.*	Bibel
bolt /bəʊlt/ *n.*	Bolzen
bulldoze /ˈbʊlˌdəʊz/ *v.*	planieren, einstampfen
bump /bʌmp/ *v.*	stoßen, anrempeln
burst /bɜːst/ *v.*	platzen
burst into /bɜːst ˈɪntə/ *v.*	ausbrechen in
carton /ˈkɑːtn/ *n.*	Getränkepackung
celebrate /ˈseləˌbreɪt/ *v.*	feiern
chibuku /tʃɪˈbuːkuː/ *n.*	*afrikanisches Bier aus Hirse und Mais*
chord /kɔːd/ *n.*	Akkord
churn /tʃɜːn/ *v.* (of the stomach: to feel as if moving, because of nervousness)	*hier:* aufgewühlt sein
churning /ˈtʃɜːnɪŋ/ *n.* (a feeling in your stomach)	mulmiges Gefühl
claws /klɔːz/ *n.*	Klauen
commotion /kəˈməʊʃn/ *n.*	Aufruhr, Tumult
concentrate /ˈkɒnsnˌtreɪt/ *v.*	sich konzentrieren
cornstalk /ˈkɔːnstɔːk/ *n.*	Maisstängel
crop /krɒp/ *n.*	Ernte

curl up /kɜːl ʌp/ *v.*	sich zusammenrollen
cymbal /ˈsɪmbl/ *n.*	Zymbel
dance routine /dɑːns ruːˈtiːn/ *n.*	Abfolge von Tanzschritten
diesel /ˈdiːzl/ *n.*	Diesel
dribble /ˈdrɪbl/ *v.* (move a ball along)	dribbeln
eagle /ˈiːgl/ *n.*	Adler
flatten /ˈflætn/ *v.*	*hier:* zertreten, platt treten
floodlights /ˈflʌdˌlaɪts/ *n.*	Flutlicht
freedom fighter /ˈfriːdəm ˈfaɪtə/ *n.*	Freiheitskämpfer
gang /gæŋ/ *n.*	Bande
harmonise /ˈhɑːmənaɪz/ *v.*	harmonieren
harmony /ˈhɑːməni/ *n.*	Harmonie, Akkord
hide /haɪd/ *n.*	Fell, Tierhaut
v.	sich verstecken
hyena /haɪˈiːnə/ *n.*	Hyäne
in cold blood /ɪn kəʊld blʌd/	kaltblütig
independently /ˌɪndɪˈpendəntli/ *adv.*	unabhängig voneinander
inspiration /ˌɪnspəˈreɪʃn/ *n.*	Inspiration, Eingebung
lead /liːd/ *n.* (an electric cable)	Stromkabel
loudspeaker /ˌlaʊdˈspiːkə/ *n.*	Lautsprecher
melody /ˈmelədi/ *n.*	Melodie
mercy /ˈmɜːsi/ *n.*	Gnade
microphone /ˈmaɪkrəˌfəʊn/ *n.*	Mikrofon
national anthem /ˈnæʃn(ə)l ˈænθəm/ *n.*	Nationalhymne
note /nəʊt/ *n.* (musical)	Note
pluck /plʌk/ *v.*	zupfen
plug in /plʌg ɪn/ *v.*	einstöpseln
pole /pəʊl/ *n.*	Stange
prey /preɪ/ *n.*	Beute
principal /ˈprɪnsəpl/ *n.*	Rektor, -in
principles /ˈprɪnsəplz/ *n.*	Grundsätze, Prinzipien
punctual /ˈpʌŋktʃuəl/ *adj.*	pünktlich
queue /kiuː/ *n.*	Schlange

relief /rɪ'liːf/ *n.*	Erleichterung
remote control /rɪ'məʊt kən'trəʊl/ *n.* (of a TV)	Fernbedienung
resent /rɪ'zent/ *v.*	ablehnen
resentment /rɪ'zentmənt/ *n.*	Ablehnung
retract /rɪ'trækt/ *v.*	*hier:* zurücklenken
rhino /'raɪnəʊ/ *n.*	Rhinozeros
sadza /sʌdzʌ/ *n.*	Weißer Mais, *Grundnahrungsmittel in Zimbabwe und anderen afrikanischen Ländern*
soul /səʊl/ *n.*	Seele
stain /steɪn/ *n.*	Fleck
stall /stɔːl/ *n.*	Stand
suspend /sə'spend/ *v.*	hängen
swoop /swuːp/ *v.*	zuschnappen
thunder /'θʌndə/ *n.*	Donner
township /'taʊnʃɪp/ *n.*	Stadtgemeinde
ululate /'juːljʊˌleɪt/ *v.*	heulen
wallet /'wɒlɪt/ *n.*	Geldbörse

Sorrow
Activities: Answer Key

Chapters 1, 2 and 3
Before you read
A. 1. c, 2. b B. 1. churning, 2. township, 3. floodlights, 4. freedom fighters C. 1. a, 2. b, 3. a

After you read
Comprehension
A. 1. c, 2. a, 3. a, 4. c B. 1. F, 2. T, 3. T, 4. T C. 1. change you, 2. cartons, 3. midday, 4. prayers
D. 1. the government, 2. the Bible, 3. Mr Sibanda, 4. to the markets

Language activities
A. 1. township, 2. floodlights, 3. classroom, 4. loudspeakers
B. 1. snake, 2. elephant, 3. giraffe, 4. eagle

What do you think?
Students' own answers

Chapters 4, 5, 6 and 7
Before you read
A. 1. b, 2. c B. 1. principles, 2. wallet, 3. hyena, 4. beggar C. 1. b, 2. b, 3. a

After you read
Comprehension
A. 1. a, 2. c, 3. c, 4. b B. 1. F, 2. T, 3. F, 4. T C. 1. steal, 2. would ride, 3. caught, 4. rubbish tip
D. 1. Rambo, 2. the beer garden, 3. Honesty, 4. Mr Sibanda

Language activities
A. 1. right - wrong, 2. rich - poor, 3. hero - coward, 4. good - bad
B. 1. strength, 2. wisdom, 3. responsibility, 4. respect

What do you think?
Students' own answers

Chapters 8, 9, 10 and 11
Before you read
A. 1. c, 2. b B. 1. curled up, 2. in cold blood, 3. soul, 4. independently
C. 1. a, 2. b, 3. b

After you read
Comprehension
A. 1. b, 2. c, 3. c, 4. a B. 1. T, 2. F, 3. T, 4. F C. 1. struggle, 2. together, 3. myself, 4. heroes
D. 1. Sorrow's schoolwork, 2. Saturday, 3. to the school, 4. Mr Sibanda's

Language activities
A. 1. sing, 2. had been, 3. were, 4. didn't B. 1. remember, 2. imagine, 3. know, 4. think

What do you think?
Students' own answers

Chapters 12, 13, 14 and 15
Before you read
A. 1. a, 2. b B. 1. burst into, 2. hide, 3. dance routine, 4. resented C. 1. b, 2. a, 3. a

After you read
Comprehension
A. 1. a, 2. b, 3. c, 4. b B. 1. F, 2. F, 3. T, 4. T C. 1. perform, 2. mud, 3. The Stardusters, 4. respect
D. 1. Dennis, 2. five minutes, 3. *Angelina*, 4. a snake

Language activities
A. 1. back-up singers, 2. electric guitar, 3. drum kit, 4. sound system
B. 1. farmers, 2. teachers, 3. musicians, 4. students

What do you think?
Students' own answers